The Great Fire
of London

STARTER LEVEL   250 HEADWORDS

Great Clarendon Street, Oxford OX2 6DP

Oxford University Press is a department of the University of Oxford.
It furthers the University's objective of excellence in research, scholarship,
and education by publishing worldwide in

Oxford New York

Auckland Cape Town Dar es Salaam Hong Kong Karachi
Kuala Lumpur Madrid Melbourne Mexico City Nairobi
New Delhi Shanghai Taipei Toronto

With offices in

Argentina Austria Brazil Chile Czech Republic France Greece
Guatemala Hungary Italy Japan Poland Portugal Singapore
South Korea Switzerland Thailand Turkey Ukraine Vietnam

OXFORD and OXFORD ENGLISH are registered trade marks of
Oxford University Press in the UK and in certain other countries

Printed in China

ACKNOWLEDGEMENTS

Illustrations by: Lyn Stone

The publisher would like to thank the following for permission to reproduce photographs: AKG-Images
p40 (Vesuvius erupting, oil on canvas); Bridgeman Art Library Ltd pp iv (The Great Fire
of London, 1799, engraved by J.C. Stadler, Louthербourg, Philippe de (1740–1812) (after)
/ Guildhall Library, City of London), 31 (View of the Monument, c.1770, James, William
(1730–80) / Private Collection / © Gavin Graham Gallery, London, UK); Getty Images p iv
(Crystal Palace fire, 1936/Popperfoto); Press Association Images p iv (Windsor Castle fire/
Fiona Hanson/PA Archive); Rex Features p45 (The Lord Mayor's Show/Nils Jorgensen).

Cover: Bridgeman Art Library Ltd (The Great Fire of London (September 1666) with Ludgate
and Old St Paul's, c.1670 (oil on canvas), English School, (17th century) / Yale Center for
British Art, Paul Mellon Collection, USA)

DOMINOES

Series Editors: Bill Bowler and Sue Parminter

The Great Fire of London

Janet Hardy-Gould

Illustrated by Lyn Stone

Janet Hardy-Gould has worked as a teacher of English for many years. In her free time she enjoys reading history books and modern novels, visiting other European countries, and drinking tea with her friends. She lives in the ancient town of Lewes in the south of England with her husband, and their two children. She has written a number of books, including *Henry VIII and his Six Wives*, and *King Arthur* in the Oxford Bookworms series, and *Mulan*, *Sinbad* and *Ibn Battuta* in the Dominoes series.

OXFORD
UNIVERSITY PRESS

BEFORE READING

1 Complete these sentences about the Great Fire of London.

a The fire happens in the year . . .

1 ☐ 1666. **2** ☐ 1936. **3** ☐ 1992.

b The fire starts . . .

1 ☐ at a baker's. **2** ☐ in the street. **3** ☐ in someone's garden.

c The fire stops . . .

1 ☐ after ten hours. **2** ☐ after five days. **3** ☐ after three months.

2 Your house is on fire! What three things do you take with you?

a . . . . **b** . . . . **c** . . . .

The Great Fire of London

Chapter 1

It is the year 1666. London is an old **city** with lots of **narrow** streets.

A lot of people are ill because there are **rats** in all the streets and the houses.

city (*plural* **cities**) a big and important town

narrow not very big

rat an animal like a big mouse; it is often dirty and can make people ill

One evening, a **baker**, Thomas Farriner, and his daughter, Harriet, are making bread.

It is late. 'We must work quickly,' says Thomas. 'We need this bread for the **King** in the morning.'

Just then, Mary, the baker's **maid**, comes in.
'You're late, Mary!' says Thomas.
'Sorry, Mr Farriner,' says Mary.

baker a person who makes bread   **king** the most important man in a country; the king here is Charles II, King of England 1660–1685   **maid** a woman who works in a rich person's house

Thomas, Harriet and Mary make bread for two hours.

Then Mr Farriner's wife, Anne, calls down to them. 'Time for bed, girls,' she says.
'We're just finishing,' says Harriet.

Harriet and Mary go up to bed. Thomas takes the bread from the **oven**.

oven this is hot and it has a door; you make things to eat in it

'Good. The **fire** is nearly **out** now,' thinks Thomas.

'Thomas!' calls Anne. 'What are you doing? It's very late.'

Thomas goes up to bed but he doesn't close the oven door.

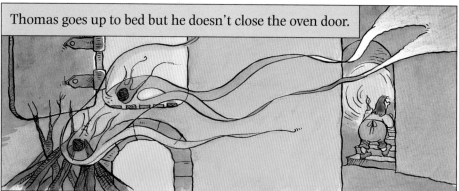

An hour later the baker's shop is **on fire**.

fire this is red and hot, and it burns   **out** not burning; with no fire   **on fire** when something is on fire, it is red, hot and burning

'**Wake up** girls! Wake up!' **cries** Anne. 'The house is on fire!'

'Quick. Open the window,' says Thomas. 'Let's go up on the **roof**.'

Thomas **jumps** to the house **next door**.

Anne and Harriet **follow** him.

But Mary stays on the roof of the baker's shop. 'Jump over here!' they all cry. 'Jump!' 'I can't,' says Mary. 'I'm afraid.'

---

wake up to stop sleeping

cry to call or say noisily

roof the top of a building

jump to move fast on your legs from one thing to a different thing

next door next to his house

follow to go after someone

READING CHECK

Match the two parts of the sentences.

a	Thomas Farriner is …	**1**	for the King.
b	Thomas makes some bread …	**2**	to bed.
c	Harriet and Mary help …	**3**	afraid.
d	Thomas doesn't close …	**4**	a baker.
e	Thomas goes up…	**5**	on fire.
f	An hour later, the shop is …	**6**	across to the next door roof.
g	Thomas, Anne and Harriet jump …	**7**	Thomas to make the bread.
h	Mary is …	**8**	the oven door.

WORD WORK

1 Find words from Chapter 1 to match the pictures.

k i n g   r _ _   c _ _ _   f _ _ _ _ _ _

m _ _ _   w _ _ _ u _   f _ _ _   n _ _ _ _ _

2 Use the words from Activity 1 to complete the sentences.

a In 1666, Charles II is the .....King.... of England.

b London is a very big ....

c Thomas Farriner and his wife .... early every morning
   to make bread for the King.

d A lot of smoke is coming from that house. Quick! It's on ....

e 'Look there's a very big mouse over there!' 'That isn't a mouse, it's a ....!'

f I'm sorry. I can't .... you onto the roof. I'm afraid!

g The old streets in this town are very ....

h Some rich people have a .... working in their house.

GUESS WHAT

What happens in the next chapter? Tick two boxes.

a ☐ Mary jumps to the next door roof.

b ☐ Mary doesn't jump because she is afraid.

c ☐ Thomas goes back to help Mary.

d ☐ Thomas, Harriet and Anne go down a ladder.

Chapter 2

People come out of their houses. They all look up at Mary. 'Jump now!' they cry.

'I can't!' says Mary. 'Please help me!'

'I'm going back,' says Thomas. 'We can't leave her. Wait here.'

'Don't go, Thomas!' cries Anne. 'Look, now this house is on fire, too.'

Just then, someone brings a **ladder**. Thomas, Anne and Harriet quickly **climb** down.

Ten minutes later . . .
'Oh mother,' says Harriet. 'Poor Mary, she's – she's dead.'
'Don't cry, my love,' says her mother.

'Look at our shop, our things, our home!' says Thomas. 'We have nothing. What can we do now?'

ladder you can go up or down tall buildings on this

climb to go up or down using your hands and feet

There is a **strong wind**, and the fire **spreads** quickly to more houses in Pudding **Lane**. 'Where are the **fire-fighters**?' everybody asks.

Just then twenty fire-fighters arrive. They begin to put water on the fire.

'Bring more water!' they cry. 'We need more water now.'

But the fire is **out of control**, and soon all the houses in Pudding Lane are on fire.

strong very fast

wind air that moves

spread to move to other houses

lane a narrow road

fire-fighter a person who stops fires

out of control when you cannot stop something or make it do what you want

The people in the street begin to ask:
'Where is the **Lord Mayor** of London?'
'He's **asleep** in bed,' says an old man.
'We want the Lord Mayor!' cry the people.

'Go and find the Lord Mayor. He lives in Maiden Lane,' says the **chief** fire-fighter to a boy. 'He must come quickly.'

'What can we do?' asks Anne. 'We can't stay here.'
'Let's go down to the **River Thames**,' cries Thomas. 'Follow me!'

Lord Mayor the most important man in London

asleep sleeping

chief the most important

river water that moves in a long line

Thames /temz/

READING CHECK

Are these sentences true or false? Tick the boxes.

		True	False
a	Mary jumps to the house next door.	☐	☑
b	Thomas wants to help Mary.	☐	☐
c	Thomas, Anne and Harriet die.	☐	☐
d	The house next to the baker's shop is soon on fire.	☐	☐
e	A hundred fire-fighters come to Pudding Lane.	☐	☐
f	Someone says, 'The Lord Mayor lives in Pudding Lane.'	☐	☐
g	Thomas, Anne and Harriet stay near the fire.	☐	☐

WORD WORK

1 **Find words from Chapter 2 in the ladder.**

2 Use the words from Activity 1 to complete these sentences.

a The Farriner family ...climb.... down the ladder.

b There is a very .... and this makes the fire worse.

c The fire .... quickly to more houses.

d Nobody can stop the fire because it is ....

e The .... fire-fighter wants to see the Lord Mayor.

f People say, 'The Lord Mayor is .... in his bed.'

g The Farriner family go down to the .... Thames.

GUESS WHAT

In the next chapter we meet Samuel Pepys. Look at his picture and tick the boxes.

Samuel Pepys ...

a ☐ is thirty-three years old.

☐ is seventy-three years old.

b ☐ works in a book shop.

☐ writes in his diary every day.

c ☐ goes to look at the fire.

☐ runs away from the fire.

1666

Chapter 3

In a different **part** of London, Samuel **Pepys** is asleep in his bed.

Pepys works for the **government**.

At home he writes a **diary** every day.

Pepys has a maid called Jane. At three o'clock in the morning she comes to his room. 'Wake up, **sir**!' she says. 'There's a fire in the city!'

---

part some, but not all of something

Pepys /piːps/

government the people who work with the king to decide what happens in the country

diary a book where you write about what happens every day

sir you say this when you talk to a rich or important man

Pepys goes to the window and looks out across London.

'It isn't a big fire,' he says to Jane. 'I'm going back to bed. Good night.'

An hour later, Jane comes back. 'Sir, there are more than three hundred houses on fire!' she cries.

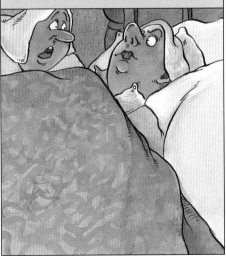

Pepys jumps out of bed. He quickly puts on his **clothes**.

clothes people wear these

'I must go to the **Tower** of London,' says Pepys. 'I can see everything from there.'

Near the Tower, Pepys meets his good friend, Richard Moore.

'What's happening?' asks Pepys.
'It's very bad **news**,' says Moore. 'There's a big fire down near the river. Everybody says it's out of control.'

They climb up the hill to the Tower. It is now six o'clock in the morning.

tower a tall building

news when someone tells you something new

16

Big **clouds** of smoke are beginning to spread across London. **Bells** are **ringing** from every **church** in the city.

'Listen to those bells!' says Moore. 'And look! Some of the houses near London **Bridge** are now on fire.'

'Let's run down to the River Thames,' cries Pepys. 'Perhaps we can help the people there.'

cloud a big white or grey thing in the sky

bell a metal thing that makes a noise when you move it

ring to make a noise like a bell

church Christian people go here to pray

bridge people can go across a river on this

17

READING CHECK

Put these sentences in the correct order. Number them 1–8.

a ☐ Pepys meets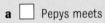

b ☐ An hour later, Jane comes back. 'Three hundred houses are on fire!' she cries.

c ☐ The fire isn't very big, and Pepys goes back to

d ☐ Moore and Pepys go down to the

e ☐ Pepys is

f ☐ Pepys quickly puts on his

g ☐ Jane wakes up Pepys. She tells him about the

h ☐ Pepys leaves the house. He goes to the

ACTIVITIES

WORD WORK

Use the words in the Tower of London to complete Pepys's diary.

Sunday, 2 September, 1666

    I am sitting and writing my **(a)**
.......diary...... . I can hear something
through my open window. All the
(b) .... in every
(c) .... in London are
(d) .... now. I can see
something through my window too. There are
(e) .... of smoke over the city.
I must put on my **(f)** .... and
go out soon. I want to climb up the
(g) .... of London and look
down on the fire! I want to walk across
London **(h)** .... and see the fire
from across the river! The King and the
(i) .... must do something to
stop the fire soon.

clouds
ringing
diary
Tower
clothes *bridge*
bells
church
government

GUESS WHAT

What happens in the next chapter? Tick the boxes.

Pepys ...

	Yes	No
a talks to the chief fire-fighter.	☐	☐
b helps the fire-fighters.	☐	☐
c goes to the Lord Mayor's house.	☐	☐
d goes to speak to the King of England.	☐	☐
e meets the Farriner family.	☐	☐

Chapter 4

Pepys and Moore arrive at the river. **Crowds** of people are running down to the river **bank**. The fire is now in the next street.

Families leave their houses with their hands **full**. They are **carrying** their things away from the fire.

Everybody wants a **boat** on the river. 'Over here!' cries a young man to the people in the boats. 'I'm first,' says an old woman.

Three people climb quickly into one of the boats. It is the Farriner family from Pudding Lane.

crowd a lot of people together

bank where you can walk next to a river

full with things in them

carry to take

boat you go across water in this

'It's Thomas Farriner from Pudding Lane,' cries a man in the crowd. 'Tell us about the fire in your baker's shop!' Thomas is **frightened**. 'I . . . I'm not a baker,' he says. 'I have a flower shop in Cat Street.'

The Farriner family leave quickly and go down the river in the boat.

Pepys and Moore walk nearer to the fire. There are clouds of smoke, and thousands of rats are in the streets. They are running from the **burning** houses.

frightened afraid   **burning** on fire

Just then, they meet twenty fire-fighters **outside** a burning building. They are putting water on the fire but it is spreading quickly.

'Can you stop the fire?' Pepys asks the chief fire-fighter.
'It's no good,' he answers. 'There's nothing we can do.'
'But you must **blow up** the buildings in front of the fire!' says Pepys. 'Then it can't spread to different parts of the city.'

'But we need to ask Thomas Bludworth, the Lord Mayor,' says the chief fire-fighter. 'Where is he?' asks Pepys. 'Nobody knows,' he answers.

outside in front of

blow up to break into small pieces noisily

'What can we do?' shouts Moore. 'We must speak to the King,' says Pepys. 'Come on. Let's find a boat. We can go up the river to Whitehall **Palace**. Perhaps we can speak to the King there.'

Pepys and Moore go quickly up the River Thames. It is eleven o'clock in the morning but the sky is black with clouds of smoke.

The wind is stronger, and many streets are now on fire. The houses on London Bridge are burning fast, and people are jumping into the river.

palace a big house where a king lives

READING CHECK

Choose the correct pictures.

a A lot of families go to the . . .

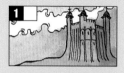  

b Some people feel . . . when they see Thomas Farriner.

c Thomas Farriner says 'I have a . . . shop.'

d In the streets there are a lot of . . .

e Pepys and Moore talk to . . .

f Pepys takes a . . . to the King's palace.

ACTIVITIES

WORD WORK

1 Find nine more words from Chapter 4 in the wordsquare.

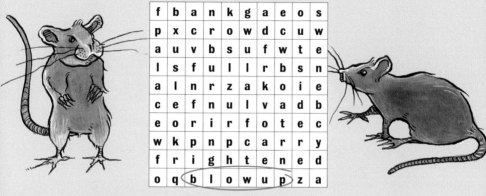

f	b	a	n	k	g	a	e	o	s
p	x	c	r	o	w	d	c	u	w
a	u	v	b	s	u	f	w	t	e
l	s	f	u	l	l	r	b	s	n
a	l	n	r	z	a	k	o	i	e
c	e	f	n	u	l	v	a	d	b
e	o	r	i	r	f	o	t	e	c
w	k	p	n	p	c	a	r	r	y
f	r	i	g	h	t	e	n	e	d
o	q	b	l	o	w	u	p	z	a

2 Use the words from Activity 1 to complete the sentences.

a The fire-fighters must stop the fire; they must .blow. up. the houses.

b We can go for a long walk on the .... of the river.

c 'Shall I .... those bags for you?' 'Yes, please, I'm very tired.'

d There's a lot of smoke in the house. Something is ....

e The children are very .... of those big dogs.

f The King lives in a very big ....

g 'Where's Richard?' 'Look, he's .... that shop over there.'

h A .... of people are waiting for the film star at the airport.

i You can travel to our country by .... or by plane.

j 'Can you open the door for me?' 'No, sorry, my hands are ....'

GUESS WHAT

What happens at the King's palace? Tick two boxes.

The King ...

a ☐ doesn't talk to Pepys.

b ☐ laughs at Pepys.

c ☐ listens carefully to Pepys.

d ☐ gives Pepys some money.

e ☐ gives Pepys a letter for the Lord Mayor.

f ☐ goes to the fire with Pepys.

Chapter 5

They arrive at the Palace of Whitehall.
'We're here to see the King,' says Pepys at the front door.

'What's your name?' asks the guard.
'Samuel Pepys.'
'Wait here, sir,' says the **guard**.

A crowd of men is standing outside the door. They are all talking excitedly.
'We must wait for rain,' says one old man.
'No, we must bring more water from the river,' says a young man.

'But we need more fire-fighters to do that!' cries a third man.

guard a man who stops people from
going into a building

'What do you two think?' the young man calls to Pepys and Moore.

Pepys walks over to the crowd of men. 'There is **only** one **solution**,' he says. 'We must blow up the buildings in front of the fire.'

Suddenly, everybody goes quiet. 'Blow up the buildings in front of the fire?' says the young man. He is **surprised**. 'Yes, that's right,' says Pepys.

Just then the guard cries: 'The King wants to see Samuel Pepys.' Now Pepys is surprised.

only not more than   **solution** the answer to a problem   **surprised** feeling that something very new is suddenly happening

Pepys goes into the King's room. '**Your Majesty**, this is Samuel Pepys,' says the guard.

'Good morning, Mr Pepys,' says the King. 'I hear you have news about the fire. Is this true?' 'Yes, Your Majesty,' says Pepys.

'The fire is now out of control, Your Majesty,' says Pepys. 'We must do something very quickly.' 'But what?' asks the King.

'The fire-fighters must blow up the houses in front of the fire,' says Pepys.

'Yes!' cries the King. 'That's the solution! We must blow up the houses. Then the fire can't spread.'

Your Majesty you say this when you talk to a king or a queen

The King writes a **letter**. 'Give this letter to Thomas Bludworth, the Lord Mayor,' he says.

'Nobody can find him,' says Pepys. 'You must find him!' says the King.

'Take one of my **coaches**. Go quickly back to the fire and find the Lord Mayor,' says the King.

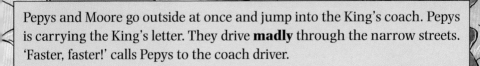

Pepys and Moore go outside at once and jump into the King's coach. Pepys is carrying the King's letter. They drive **madly** through the narrow streets. 'Faster, faster!' calls Pepys to the coach driver.

letter a piece of paper with writing on it; you send it to someone   **coach** a kind of car with horses   **madly** quickly and without thinking

READING CHECK

Choose the correct words to complete these sentences.

a At the door of the palace, Pepys talks to a guard. maid.

b Outside the palace, Pepys meets a crowd of women. men.

c Moore Pepys talks to the King.

d The King wants doesn't want to blow up the houses.

e The King gives Pepys a letter. bag of money.

f The King wants Pepys to find the Lord Mayor. the chief fire-fighter.

g Pepys goes back to the fire in the King's boat. coach.

WORD WORK

1 Find words from Chapter 5 in these sentences and complete the puzzle below.

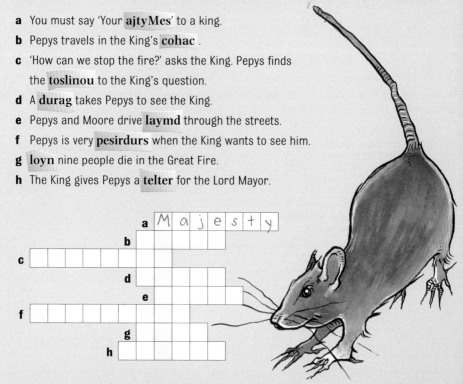

a You must say 'Your **ajtyMes**' to a king.

b Pepys travels in the King's **cohac** .

c 'How can we stop the fire?' asks the King. Pepys finds
the **toslinou** to the King's question.

d A **durag** takes Pepys to see the King.

e Pepys and Moore drive **laymd** through the streets.

f Pepys is very **pesirdurs** when the King wants to see him.

g **loyn** nine people die in the Great Fire.

h The King gives Pepys a **telter** for the Lord Mayor.

		a	M	a	j	e	s	t	y		
	b										
c											
	d										
		e									
f											
	g										
	h										

2 Read the blue squares and write down the name of the high building on page 31.

GUESS WHAT

What happens in the next chapter? Tick the boxes.

a Pepys is angry with . . .

1 ☐ Richard Moore.

2 ☐ the Lord Mayor.

3 ☐ the chief fire-fighter.

b Who writes about the fire in his diary?

1 ☐ the King.

2 ☐ Thomas Farriner.

3 ☐ Samuel Pepys.

c The fire burns for . . .

1 ☐ one more day.

2 ☐ three more days.

3 ☐ one more week.

d The fire burns . . .

1 ☐ 300 houses.

2 ☐ 3,000 houses.

3 ☐ 13,000 houses.

The _ _ _ _ _ _ _ _ _ (1669) to remember the Great Fire of London. You can walk up it today.

Chapter 6

In the end, Pepys finds the Lord Mayor. 'Ah, here you are!' Pepys cries angrily. 'Everybody is looking for you!'

'Hello, Pepys,' says the Lord Mayor. 'I'm very **tired** – I must sit down.'

'Here is a letter from the King,' says Pepys. 'You must blow up the buildings in front of the fire.'

'I know,' says the Lord Mayor. 'I want to **pull down** houses near the fire but nobody listens to me. People don't want to lose their homes.'

tired you feel tired when you need to sit down or sleep

pull down to make a building come down

Just then some of the King's **soldiers** arrive.

'Lord Mayor, we are here to blow up houses,' says one of the soldiers.

'Yes,' says the Lord Mayor. 'Good luck! I'm going home now. I'm tired and dirty, and I want to change my clothes.'

'But . . . Lord Mayor. Wait!' call the soldiers.

'Goodbye,' says the Lord Mayor.

The men blow up some houses but they are very near to the fire. 'It's no good,' says Pepys to the soldiers. 'You must blow up buildings one street away from the fire.'

The soldiers pull down houses and blow up shops. It is now nine o'clock on Sunday evening. Pepys and Moore go home.

soldier a person in an army

For three more days the **Great** Fire of London **burns**. Frightened people and hungry rats run madly through the streets.

The fire spreads to the most important houses and churches in the city. Old St Paul's **Cathedral** burns day and night.

Day after day the fire-fighters . . .

. . . and soldiers work to stop the fire.

great very big or important   **burn** to be on fire   **cathedral** a big important church

On the fourth day the wind changes **direction** and the fire slowly stops. The fire-fighters stand and watch for the first time in days.

Many people come back to look for their houses and shops but they find nothing.

At home Pepys begins to write about the fire in his diary. He knows the government must work a lot to help the people of London.

direction where something is going

Five days later, Pepys and Moore climb up the tower of the last church in the **centre** of London.

They look over the city.
'What a black day,' says Pepys. 'Over thirteen thousand houses and ninety churches . . . and now there is nothing.'
'Don't feel bad about that,' says Moore. '**Instead** let's remember something important. Only nine people are dead.'

centre the part in the middle   **instead** in the place of something

Fifty years later London is a very different city. There are no more old narrow streets in the city centre, but beautiful **wide** streets instead. And a new St Paul's Cathedral stands not far from the banks of the River Thames. But the most important thing is . . .

. . . there are no more rats.

wide not narrow

ACTIVITIES

READING CHECK

Choose the right words to finish the sentences.

a When the soldiers arrive, the Lord
Mayor goes . . .

   1 ☑ home.

   2 ☐ to the King's palace.

   3 ☐ to the Tower of London.

b At first the soldiers blow up buildings . . .

   1 ☐ in the fire.

   2 ☐ very near the fire.

   3 ☐ one street away from the fire.

c St Paul's Cathedral . . .

   1 ☐ burns for a long time.

   2 ☐ burns for a short time.

   3 ☐ isn't in the fire.

d After four days the wind . . .

   1 ☐ stops.

   2 ☐ changes direction.

   3 ☐ becomes stronger.

e In the Great Fire of London . . .

   1 ☐ nine people die.

   2 ☐ ninety people die.

   3 ☐ nine hundred people die.

f Fifty years later London has . . .

   1 ☐ a new cathedral.

   2 ☐ a lot of rats.

   3 ☐ beautiful narrow streets.

WORD WORK

1 Find the words from Chapter 6.

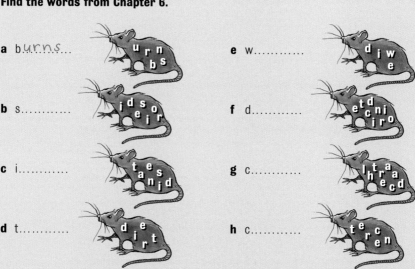

a b u r n s

b s

c i

d t

e w

f d

g c

h c

2 Use the words from Activity 1 to complete the sentences.

a The Great Fire of London …burns… for five days.

b A church is smaller than a ……………… .

c The Lord Mayor is very ……………… and he wants to go to sleep.

d The fire-fighters can't stop the fire by pulling down houses; they must blow up the houses ……………… .

e The wind changes ……………… after four days and the fire stops.

f A ……………… is a person who works in the army.

g The new ……………… of London has beautiful ……………… streets.

GUESS WHAT

What happens to Samuel Pepys after the fire? Tick two boxes.

a ☐ He meets and loves the King's daughter.

b ☐ The King gives him a big house and a lot of money.

c ☐ He becomes an important person in the government.

d ☐ After the fire he stops working and is a very poor man.

e ☐ He is the next Lord Mayor of London.

f ☐ Lots of people read about the fire in his diary hundreds of years later.

PROJECT A *Famous Disasters*

1 Use the words in the box to complete this news report about the Eruption of Mount Vesuvius.

> boats   burning   city   clouds   crowds
> direction   frightened   jump   letter   on fire

24 AUGUST, 79

VESUVIUS IS ERUPTING

Mount Vesuvius is erupting. **(a)**.................... rocks are falling on the **(b)**.................... of Pompeii below. The sky is black with **(c)**.................... of ash, and the city is **(d)**.................... **(e)**.................... of **(f)**.................... people are running from their houses. They are running in the **(g)**.................... of the sea and waiting for **(h)**.................... to take them away.

From the town of Misenum across the sea, Pliny the younger is writing about the disaster in a **(i)**.................... to a friend. His uncle, Pliny the older, tells all the boats to go across the sea. Pliny the older is going with them to help the people in Pompeii.

Twenty thousand people **(j)**.................... into boats and get away. But Pliny the older and over two thousand people are left in the burning city. They are all dead under the burning rocks and ash.

PROJECTS

2 Use the information in Activity 1 to complete the table.

DISASTER NAME	The Eruption of Vesuvius
WHERE AND WHEN?	
WHAT IS HAPPENING?	
WHAT ARE PEOPLE DOING?	
WHAT IS PLINY THE YOUNGER DOING?	
WHAT IS PLINY THE OLDER DOING?	
HOW MANY PEOPLE GET AWAY?	
HOW MANY ARE DEAD?	

3 Complete this table about the Great Fire of London.

DISASTER NAME	The Great Fire of London
WHERE AND WHEN?	
WHAT IS HAPPENING?	
WHAT ARE PEOPLE DOING?	
WHAT ARE THE FIRE-FIGHTERS DOING?	
WHAT IS PEPYS DOING?	
HOW MANY ARE DEAD?	

**4 Now write a news report about the Great Fire of London.
Begin your report like this.**

3 September 1666
   This is the second day of the fire and the city of London is burning.

41

PROJECT B *Conversations about The Fire*

1 Who are these people from *The Great Fire of London*? Match the two parts of the sentences.

a Thomas Farriner . . .

b Mary . . .

c Anne Farriner . . .

d Samuel Pepys . . .

e Charles II . . .

f Thomas Bludworth . . .

g Harriet Farriner . . .

h Jane . . .

i Richard Moore . . .

1 is the baker's wife.

2 is the baker's maid.

3 is the baker's daughter.

4 is the Lord Mayor of London.

5 is the baker to the King.

6 works for the government and writes in his diary every day.

7 is Samuel Pepys's maid.

8 is Samuel Pepys's good friend.

9 is the King of England.

2 Use these words to complete this conversation.

| girls remember shop smoke talking wake where |

ANNE **(a)** . . . . up Thomas! There's a fire!

THOMAS A fire? **(b)** . . . . is it?

ANNE I think it's down in the **(c)** . . . .

There's a lot of **(d)** . . . . on the stairs.

THOMAS Oh no! I **(e)** . . . . now! The oven door!

ANNE What are you **(f)** . . . . about?

THOMAS Oh, it's not important.

ANNE Quick. Let's go and tell the **(g)** . . . .

Come on!

3 Here's another conversation. What does Pepys say? Complete the conversation.

Well, what are the fire-fighters doing?

Yes, I can see it. But it's only small.

OK. OK. I'm going to the Tower to have a look.

A fire? Where?

It's not important Jane. Go back to bed.

JANE	Wake up, sir! There's a fire in the city.
PEPYS	**(a)** ....
JANE	Over there. Look out of the window.
PEPYS	**(b)** ....
JANE	But it's spreading very fast, sir.
PEPYS	**(c)** ....
JANE	Back to bed sir? I'm afraid! The fire is out of control.
PEPYS	**(d)** ....
JANE	They are putting water on the fire, but the wind is making the fire stronger.
PEPYS	**(e)** ....

4 Choose one of these pictures from the story. Write the conversation.

5 Now read your conversation with a friend.

GRAMMAR CHECK

Present Simple: affirmative and negative

We make most Present Simple affirmative verbs with the infinitive without *to*.
We add –s or –es to make the third person singular form.

Just then Mary comes in.   *Thomas goes up to bed.*

We make most third person Present Simple negative verbs with doesn't/don't + infinitive without *to*.

He doesn't close the oven door.   *They don't live next to the river.*

The Present Simple affirmative of be → is/are, and the Present Simple negative of be → isn't/aren't.

The fire isn't very big.   *All the houses are on fire.*

1 Put the verbs in brackets into the Present Simple – affirmative or negative.

Today, London a) ...**has**... (have) a
very important mayor: the Lord Mayor
of London. Every year, there is a 'Lord
Mayor's Show'. The new Lord Mayor
b) .... (go) through the streets of
the old centre of London. Of course, the
Lord Mayor c) .... (not walk). He
d) .... (drive) in a wonderful old
coach with beautiful horses! And he

e) .... (not wear) usual clothes. He f) .... (put on) a red coat and a big
black hat.

The show g) .... (begin) at 11 o'clock in the morning and the Lord Mayor
h) .... (move) slowly through the streets in his coach for about three hours. Many
people from different countries i) .... (come) to watch, but they j) .... (not
know) the Lord Mayor's name because he k) .... (not be) a very famous person!
All the people at the Lord Mayor's Show l) .... (have) an exciting time. The show
m) .... (finish) at 5 o'clock with lots of fireworks over the River Thames. The Lord
Mayor n) .... (watch) the fireworks and then o) .... (say) goodbye to the
crowd.

GRAMMAR CHECK

Modal auxiliary verbs: must

We use must + infinitive without *to* when we think it is necessary or very important to do something, or when it is an obligation.

I must go to the Tower of London.

She must climb down the ladder.

We must help the people of London.

2 Complete the sentences with *must* and the verbs in the box.

| blow up | come | help | jump | arrive | sit down | speak |

a You ..must jump.. to the house next door, Mary!

b The fire-fighters .... quickly.

c Where is the Lord Mayor? He .... here soon to see the fire!

d I .... to the King of England! It's very important.

e I'm very tired. I .... in a chair.

f We .... the houses in front of the fire.

g The government .... the people of London.

3 Write the words in the correct order to make sentences.

a the / bread / King / must / they / make / for / nice
..They must make nice bread for the King...

b fire-fighters / find / more / water / the / must
....

c must / out / Pepys / of / quickly / jump / bed
....

d now / house / must / leave / I / the
....

e the / find / a / you / on / boat / river / must
....

GRAMMAR

Subject and object pronouns

We use subject pronouns – I, you, he, she, it, we, and they – to replace subject nouns. Subject pronouns go in front of the main verb.

Mary helps to bake bread. She helps to bake bread.

The Mayor isn't here. He is asleep.

We use object pronouns – me, you, him, her, it, us, and them – to replace object nouns. Object pronouns go after the main verb. They can also go after prepositions.

That's the baker! I know him.   Where are the guards? I can't see them.

Pepys finds the King and he speaks to him.

4 Choose the correct word to complete the sentences.

a London is an old city. **It**/**He** has lots of narrow streets.

b There are rats in all the streets and the houses. People don't like **they/them**!

c An old woman gets into a boat. **She/Her** is frightened.

d Samuel Pepys is in bed. **Him/He** is asleep.

e The fire is very bad. The fire-fighters must stop **it/them**.

f 'I want to see Pepys,' says the King. 'Bring him to **I/me**.'

5 Complete the sentences. Use the subject and object pronouns in the box.

he	her	it	you	I	they
she	them	him	you		

a Harriet is sixteen. ...She... lives over a shop. Many young men like ....

b The baker starts the fire. Everybody is angry with............, so .... runs away.

c The rats run through the streets. .... are very big and nobody likes ....!

d 'Are .... afraid of the fire?' 'Yes, ... am!'

e Please open this letter from the King. He wants .... to read .... now.

47

GRAMMAR

GRAMMAR CHECK

Adjectives: order before nouns

We use adjectives to describe nouns. Adjectives go in front of a noun.

London has old, narrow streets.

When there is more than one adjective, we put the adjective that gives our opinion first.

an interesting, new cathedral   *a nice, big, green boat.*

We usually put adjectives in this order:

1 Opinion	2 Size	3 Age	4 Shape	5 Colour	6 Nationality
wonderful	big	old	narrow	blue	English
good	little	new	wide	red	French

6 Write the words in the correct order to make sentences.

  a great / English / he's / writer / a *He's a great English writer.*

  b maid / a / new / nice / she's ....

  c rats / brown / they're / long ....

  d old / he's / bad / mayor / a ....

  e a / man / he's / young / tall ....

7 What can people see 50 years after the Great Fire of London? Put the words in brackets in the correct order and write sentences.

  a There are a lot of streets. (wide / nice / big)

    There are a lot of nice, big, wide streets.

  b There's a cathedral. (white / beautiful)

    ....

  c There are some shops. (French / new / wonderful)

    ....

  d There's a bridge. (narrow / old)

    ....

  e There are a lot of houses. (red / new / nice)

    ....

GRAMMAR CHECK

Everybody, everything, nobody, nothing, somebody, and something

We use everybody and everything to talk about 'all the people' and 'all the things'.

Everybody wants a boat on the river.   *I can see everything from here.*

We use nobody and nothing to talk about 'no person or people' or 'no thing or things'.

Nobody listens to me.   *We have nothing.*

We use somebody and something to talk about an unknown person or thing.

Somebody brings a ladder.   *We must do something about the fire.*

8 **Write the sentences again. Use *everybody, everything, nobody, nothing, somebody,* or *something*.**

a All the people must leave the city. ..*Everybody must leave the city.*..

b No person can stop the fire. ....

c There's a person on the roof! ....

d We must take all the things out of our house. ....

e After the fire, there's not one thing left in the centre of London.

....

f I can see a thing in the river. ....

9 **Complete the dialogue with the words in the box.**

somebody	everybody	nobody	nothing	~~something~~

King Mr Pepys, you know a) ..*something*.. about the fire. Please tell me.

Pepys Your Majesty, the fire is out of control. We must blow up the houses in front of it.

King Oh dear! b) .... must find the Lord Mayor quickly.

Pepys Yes, Your Majesty, but c) .... can find him!

King Take one of my coaches now. Oh, and Pepys – is the cathedral all right?

Pepys No, Your Majesty, d) .... is safe and e) .... is frightened. The fire is very big.

49

GRAMMAR CHECK

Suffixes: –ed and –ing

We can add the suffixes –ed and –ing to a verb or noun to make some adjectives.

Adjectives with –ed usually describe how somebody feels.

Mary is frightened of the fire.

Samuel Pepys is in bed because he is tired.

Adjectives with –ing usually describe something.

The fire is frightening.

His work is very tiring.

10 **Choose the correct word to complete the sentences.**

a The Lord Mayor is **tired**/tiring because he always sleeps badly.

b Samuel Pepys's diary is very **interested/interesting**.

c The men are **excited/exciting** when they meet the King.

d People are **surprised/surprising** about the number of houses on fire.

e The fire is spreading. It's very **frightened/frightening**.

f Are you **interested/interesting** in the King's palace?

g The news about the fire isn't **surprised/surprising**.

11 **Complete the sentences with the correct adjectives.**

a London is a very in .teresting. city.

b Mary is too fr............ to jump to the house next door.

c Pepys is in............ in the Great Fire of London.

d Making bread is ti............ work.

e The fire in Pudding Lane is fr............ .

f The King is su............ because nobody can find the Lord Mayor.

g Harriet and Mary go up to bed because they are ti............ .

h The crowd at the Palace of Whitehall are ex............ .

GRAMMAR

GRAMMAR CHECK

Plural nouns

We usually add –s to singular nouns to make plural nouns.

maid – maids   bridge – bridges   river – rivers

When a noun ends in –sh, –ch, –s, –ss, –x, or –z, we add –es to make the plural.

bus – buses   dress – dresses   watch – watches   box – boxes

When a noun ends in a consonant + –y, we change the y to i and add –es.

country – countries   story – stories   family – families

Some nouns have irregular plurals.

man – men   woman – women   child – children   person – people

2 Complete the sentences with a plural noun. Use the words in the box.

child	church	city	coach	day	diary	person

a The ..children.. run away from the fire.

b In 1666, London is one of the biggest .... in the world.

c When the fire begins, all the bells ring in the

....

d Pepys and Moore drive through the streets in
one of the King's ....

e The Great Fire of London stops after five

....

f Only nine .... die in the Great Fire of
London.

g Samuel Pepys's .... are now very famous books.

3 Correct the text.

When the fire begins, all the a) <del>persons</del> *people* run out of their b) housses to see it. The
c) boyes and d) girles are frightened. Everybody tells e) storys about the burning city.
When the fire gets worse, all the f) ratts come out of the g) buildinges, too. The
h) mans, i) womans and j) childs of London all run through the k) streetes to the
l) bankes of the River Thames. Two or three m) familys jump into n) boatts and they
go down the river, away from the fire.

Dominoes is an enjoyable series of illustrated classic and modern stories in four carefully graded language stages – from Starter to Three – which take learners from beginner to intermediate level.

Each *Domino* reader includes:
- **a good story** to read and enjoy
- **integrated activities** to develop reading skills and increase active vocabulary
- **personalized projects** to make the language and story themes more meaningful
- **seven pages of grammar activities** for consolidation.

Each *Domino* pack contains a reader, plus a MultiROM with:
- **a complete audio recording of the story**, fully dramatized to bring it to life
- **interactive activities** to offer further practice in reading and language skills and to consolidate learning.

If you liked this Starter Level *Domino*, why not read these?

William Tell and Other Stories
Retold by John Escott

'The men and the women in this book – William Tell, Tom Blood, Lord Bao, King Matthias, Johnny Appleseed, and Lady Godiva – are all real people from history.

But every time someone tells an old story, they change things in it, to make them bigger, better, and more exciting. So what is true in this book and what is not? Read all six of the stories, and see what you think.

Book ISBN: 978 0 19 424703 0
MultiROM Pack ISBN: 978 0 19 424667 5

Tristan and Isolde
Retold by Bill Bowler

Tristan and Isolde are in love, but Isolde must marry King Mark. So a happy love story seems impossible . . .

The lovers meet every day but then, one night, King Mark finds them together. Now Tristan must leave the castle, but he is badly hurt and dying. Only Isolde can help him.

Can Isolde find Tristan in time? Can their love survive?

Book ISBN: 978 0 19 424713 9
MultiROM Pack ISBN: 978 0 19 424677 4

You can find details and a full list of books in the *Dominoes* catalogue and Oxford English Language Teaching Catalogue, and on the website: www.oup.com/elt

Teachers: see www.oup.com/elt for a full range of online support, or consult your local office.

	CEF	Cambridge Exams	IELTS	TOEFL iBT	TOEIC
Starter	A1	YLE Movers	–	–	–
Level 1	A1–A2	YLE Flyers/KET	3.0	–	–
Level 2	A2–B1	KET-PET	3.0-4.0	–	–
Level 3	B1	PET	4.0	57-86	550